HAPPY BIRTHDAY!
(you poor old wreck)

Edited by Helen Exley

Andrew Broady, 8

EXLEY
NEW YORK · WATFORD, UK

To Dalton and Momtom and everyone else
who should be too old to believe in birthdays.

Titles in this series:
Grandmas and Grandpas
To Dad
To Mum

Published simultaneously in 1992 by Exley Publications Ltd. in Great Britain, and Exley Giftbooks in the USA.

Published in Great Britain in 1984
Exley Publications Ltd, 16 Chalk Hill, Watford, Herts WD1 4BN, United Kingdom.
Exley Giftbooks, 232 Madison Avenue, Suite 1206, NY 10016, USA.

Second and third printings 1985
Fourth printing 1986
Fifth and sixth printings 1988
Seventh printing 1989
Eighth printing 1990
Ninth and tenth printings 1992
Eleventh, twelfth and thirteenth printings 1993
Fourteenth printing 1994
Fifteenth printing 1995

Front cover illustration by Leeanne Jenkins
Back cover illustration by Elem Jones
Printed and bound by Oriental Press, U.A.E.

Happy Birht-Day

Samantha

3

What is a birthday?

You have a birthday every year and you can be any age and you start with being one second old.

Emma Labrum, 7

Emma Labram, 7

Just think, if only you could snap your fingers on the birthday you wanted and never grow any older. HUH! Birthdays won't even let you do that because you've got so much artheritis your fingers won't snap!

Susan Curzon, 12

Growing old means that you can be young and then old but you can't grow old and then young.

Colin West, 8

Cats have birthdays like us. No one nose what cats thik about birthdays probly nothink.

Denis Hutchinson, 8

I think it is a good idea to celebrate our birthdate to keep track of how old one is otherwise we would be in an awful mess. *Christopher Fuller, 11*

Take my advice and ignore birthdays unless you want to end up old and wrinkled. *Susan Curzon, 12*

Nigel Bosley, 10

Birthdays are when you get up very early and you are sent back to bed.
Juliet Bowman, 12

Birthday

Remembered by the young.
"Forgotten" by anyone over thirty-five.
It is a looming storm cloud or an island paradise in a young life.
It happens about half a billion times a year,
And is free.
A. Martin, 13

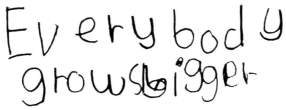

lexander Davenport, 5

Birthdays!

When your mother arrives home from shopping you are there waiting for her, for the first time all year, offering to unpack her bags, which she politely declines. You later sneak up to her room and peep at the interesting package under her bed and find a rain-soaked train set. You get to school late next morning because you've overslept. Your teacher promptly informs you that you are going to have to stay after school. You think "typical".

The rest of the day drags on forever until finally the last bell rings. You rush out of class, run down the stairs, trip over the bottom step, fall down and get a nose bleed. You race home in the pouring rain to a mother who is still smiling even though her new hairstyle has been ruined by the pouring rain. She lets you have a coke and far more chocolate chips than is good for you. Then you eat a large dinner and more cake than you can possibly eat (but you eat it anyway). You spend the rest of the evening trying to make the train work and go to bed feeling very sick.

Graham Munday, 13

Claire Billinghurst, 8

6

I can't wait till my Birthday,
Eating ice cream and birthday cakes
Gobble gobble. *Imraan Esmail, 11 and three days*

Birthdays are nice because you can fight your brother
and he gets the blame. *Mark Scull, 11*

When it's my birthday I go bananas. Birthdays are
the best they're crazy crazy. *Gregory Yeomans, 10*

I always feel superior over people one year younger
than myself, but if someone is one year older than me
I feel small and look forward to when I will be one
year older, but everyone else seems to get one year
older as well. *Steven McMullan, 11*

Amber Lodhi, 5

A birthday is happiness all the world over.

Zoltan Kovari, 9

From cradle to grave

0 I wish I could be one week old once again. You only had to cry if you wanted something done, just like shouting zap, everything is done. No worrying about homework, you just sit gurgling merrily at home. *Elizabeth Wyatt, 9*

Harriet Lee, 9

2 My best age is 2. Everybody is kind and almost never gets mad. When you go out you are pushed along or carried. You never have to clean your bedroom or make your bed. And you can crawl into places you aren't supposed to go.
Sarah Hill, 9

Nuala Roberts, 11

8 The best age I have ever been is eight. I liked it because nobody ever said "You are two old for this" or "You are too young for that". Another reason why I liked being eight was that I felt very grown up. I do not feel grown up any more although I still feel quite a bit older than people who are eight. *Sophie McMullen, 9*

Sarah Morris, 9

11 The age I would like to be, is the age I am now. I am enjoying being eleven very much. When you're eleven you can have fun, make a noise and get dirty without people thinking it peculiar; if a grown up did things like this it would be considered silly. I like doing new things, such as seeing a play for the first time, visiting new places, buying new things, which when I'm older will not be new and not so interesting. I have more things to look forward to, going abroad by myself, going to X-rated films, having more grown-up hairstyles, staying up later. I am quite content to stay eleven. *Harriet Wootliff, 11*

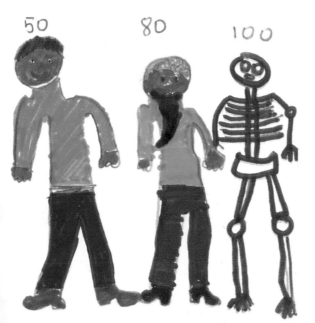

James Barker, 9

13 At thirteen I would begin being a teenager. This is the age I most look forward to. You are neither a child nor an adult. This means life can be fun. You are old enough to decide for yourself but not old enough to have problems. *Jean Davis, 10*

Sweet sixteen and many more 💙 Kisses too.
Catherine Thompson

17 I think the ideal age is seventeen, because you will have finished school. You could stay up late and watch horror films. *Clara McAlinden, 10*

19 I think 19 will be my nicest age. Then I will be rich enough to own a Jaguar, a Rolls Royce and a Mercedes. *Merry Lomax, 9*

21 Birthdays are happy times until . . . you reach the biggest birthday, "The perfect age", Twenty-one! Then every birthday is harder to hide. A slight crease under the eyes and then you're not twenty-one. You're old. *Sara Burnham, 13*

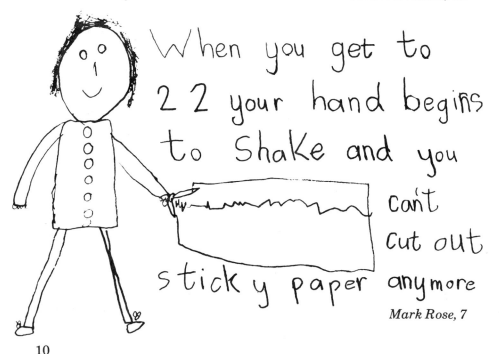

When you get to 2 2 your hand begins to shake and you can't cut out sticky paper anymore

Mark Rose, 7

23 I would like to be about twenty-three because you are too young to have a family and too old to be fussed over by relatives.   *Lowri Vernon Roberts, 10*

24 It would be good to stay at twenty-four. At twenty-four all the boys would be proposing marriage to me and carrying my shopping bags and take off their hats to me. They would try to win me with flattery and compliments, like saying I was the most beautiful girl in the world, I was like a gem and a sweet smelling fragrant flower.   *Maria Richards, 11*

WHEN I am 24 I will BE old I will Go To THE NURSE She gives ME a Walking Stick.

Joanne McKinley, 6

I think I will stay with 24, a much nicer age. I might even be married (every age has snags to it).
Jane Moriarty, 11

25 When you are about 25 you can do everything. But you also got to do the shopping and do the dirty work like washing dishes and the smelly shorts.   *David Loney, 9*

Middle age is wen you Pors yor Drivin test

Emma Newman, 7

40 Then we turn forty, by this time we lose half our strength and we start to put on weight.

Daniel Lehane, 11

Today is my fortieth birthday, and I am beginning to look it. It's quite an ordeal to look at my face first thing in the morning. I wouldn't dare leave my bedroom with my make-up off. I might give someone a terrible scare. Not that I look all that glamorous with my make-up on. I suppose the trouble with me is that I am too scared to admit that I'm middle-aged. Too scared to face the fact that when I stop laughing the wrinkles don't go.

Belinda Harding, 14

I am forty, I am turning old. I just retired from my job because I cannot manage going up and down hills. I know I will soon die.

Jennifer Turner, 8

Dolores Mahon, 8

Your legs begin to ache and you feel you'll collapse When you an are about 42.

Patrick Gaughan, 8

Top left: Tara Mercer; top right: Samantha King
Bottom left: Paul Walsh; bottom right: William Wells

50 When old people are 50 years old they start getting crincals.
Suzanne Everitt, 9

When you turn 50 years old, your bones get creaky.
Dean Hodges, 9

Andrew Hammond, 10

The only disadvantage when you are 50 or over, the brain tissue gets smaller and you start to become a litle screwy.
Mark Tychnoisky, 11

When you have a birthday at the age of fifty you feel terrible.
David Huggett, 10

55 When you are about 55 your bones start going very soft and just about holds you up. *Darren Penn*

When I am 55 I will not be able to walk.
Mark Dyson, 10

60 When you are 60 you can't have birthday partys and you cannot go to school and run and jump, skip and play.
Andrew Roddie, 10

Sixty is quite a pleasant age because you have grandchildren to spoil and buy things for. You would go on exotic journeys to Europe and the Orient. You would have to be really cheerful though because you might die the next day.
Erica Sabine, 10

70 One of the saddest things of growing old is that you might have an illness that cannot be cured and the doctor might say, "We are sorry, very, very, but we are going to have to put you to sleep."
Alex Stanger, 7

100 I wonder what it's like on your one hundreth birthday. You might get cards from important people.
Far out! Well I'm only twelve and I've got a long wait.

Andrea Hurley, 12

I would like to be the grand age of 100. I would like to feel I have lived a century, seen children grow up, the world changed, peace made between people who hate each other.

E. Swallow

Mark Sully, 10

136 I would like to live till am 136 years old because I can be in the book of records.

Norma Valentine, 10

PS. A final thought

When you die you don't have birthdays.   *David Pollick, 7*

PPS.

I would like to tell you one more thing, the middle age always win.

Penny Sullings, 9

15

Oh to be a grown-up!

I like the idea of growing old, well, not too old, about nineteen or so.   *Mimi Cuthbert, 9*

I like growing up because when you grow up you don't have to do what your mother says.   *Jason Torrington, 9*

Wayne Miles, 9

I think the pleasures of growing old are when you could get out of school and get married and have children.   *Julia Lappin*

I am glad that when you are old, you do not have to do homework. I am very very glad about that.

Elizabeth Fisher, 8

I never want to be a grown up. The only things I look forward to are being able to smoke legally, have sex legally, drink alcohol legally, drive, get into X-rated films legally and stay out till any time I like. Oh, and also getting more money. I could marry a millionaire, but I rather think I'll want to work instead.　*Alison, 14*

I want to be a grown up because then I won't have to eat things that are good for me all the time.

Jaynie Hoffman, 10

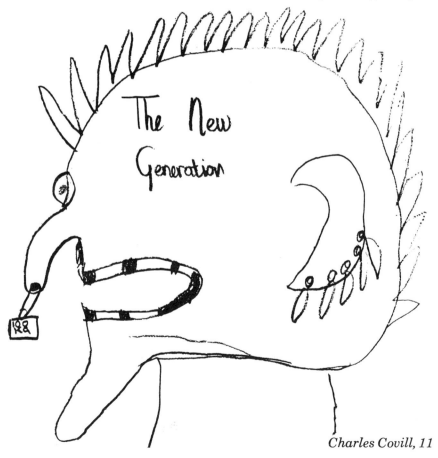

The New Generation

Charles Covill, 11

'Before' . . . and 'after'

The disadvantage of being old is not looking as good as you did when you were young. It is like looking in a before and after picture but the other way around.

Gino Miele, 10

me how

me when I'm old

James Hooker, 9

Old age begins at 8

When I started jogging I was three. But I can't jog so much now as I used to.   *Maxine Brown, 8*

Everyone has a birthday each year. You are a year older, and your body gets weaker. People get weaker every year. I wouldn't like to be old. It means a lot of trouble for the young people. I soon will be an old person. I am only nine.   *Lisa Beagle, 9*

About the birthday longest ago that I can remember is when I was seven, and that wasn't very long ago. I got about fifteen presents then and everyone loved me, now look at me. I used to have parties with lots of people there, but now I can only invite a couple of friends over and we go to McDonald's or somewhere.   *Nicholas, 10*

When you have a birthday you feel miserable because you don't get toy cars anymore.

Michael Graham, 8

Year by Year
And day by day
I'm growing older
And so I say;
I'm not as young as I'd like to be,
But in this world, who is?

Janet Smith, 13

Michael Graham, 8

Amber Jones, 7

Grown-up just means bossy

Grown-ups are like Big children, only they are bossier and they say they are always right. *Marianne Wales, 10*

Grown-ups always decide what we'll have to eat and they always seem to pick the thing that I do not like! I do not like the way that they treat you like worms.
Heather Dean, 10

When children want to say something to adults while they are talking they tell the children not to interrupt, but it seems an awful long time until they stop talking and listen to you. *Clare Theakson, 10*

I do not like being called "little girl". The way adults say it makes it sound like I was only four.
Elizabeth Schofield, 11

grown up
is when
you can boss
children around

Caroline H. Grant, 8

Sara Brudenell, 7

23

Middle-age fossils

Middle age is when you start watching boring things like the News.
Scott Dustan, 10

Middle age people work all day, washing the dishes and vacuuming. At night they watch the television and eat pizzas.
Sharon Stables, 10

When you get to middle age you start doing things, like smoking, sleeping in the afternoon, nagging and so on.
Anthony Trigg, 11

The good things about being middle aged is lying in bed, watching horror films.
Keith Rettie, 10

Middle-aged people get bad-tempered very easily. Maybe they think they are past the best in life.
Toni Denman

when you have a
birthday and you are
middle aged your
friends all clink their
glasses and cheer
and it gives you a
headache.
Philip Brooke 8

Some times grown ups
can be a real pain
and very trubblesome
if they want
to be.

Leyla Mehmet, 8

Imraan Esmail, 11

Grown-ups!

Some adults do the most crazy things like going up a mountain and getting stuck in some mud, and then some more people come along and get stuck in the same lot of mud.   *Marianne Wales, 10*

Most grown-ups get married, have children and then get deforced and get married again.   *Kerstie Dent, 11*

Grown up people have more chances to do things because children cannot spank grown up people.
Aike Arnheim, 7

Grown-ups are always rushing around doing things like sweeping up last minute bits of dust off the floor and rushing everywhere shooing children away to school, not to mention trying to sing a baby to sleep before rushing off to a PTA meeting or running to the grocery store at closing time.   *Georgina Morgan, 8*

When grown-ups are buying things they always change their minds. When they ask my opinion, if I said, "Yes buy it", they don't.
Katherine Vickers, 10

Grown-ups are children which have grown.
Anne Surtees Dawson, 10

Leyla, 8

Some grown-ups act like two-year olds
Rachel Bouness, 10

old people die When
They are very very
old Like 50 or 40
ZARA   BANNERJEE   5 YEARS

That dreaded 30th birthday

The first sign of growing old is needing a pair of glasses which reveals the second and third signs, the first wrinkle and the first white hair. The fourth sign is the thirtieth birthday.

Agnes Ring, 15

Middle age is when you can drive a car and have a baby.

Caroline H. Grant

People don't like telling you their real age when they turn thirty. They say silly things like, "I'm only 21".

Manuel Reveiz, 11

Suddenly life is a lot harder. You become middle-aged. You get "middle-age spread". You go flabby around your waist. You do not feel quite as young and fit as you used to. Your hair either starts to go white or to fall out. Or both! But you are still growing in two ways. You are growing older and, probably, fatter.

Luisa Kate Davis, 12

Can you hear me?
Your going deaf,
what a shame.
Can you see me
or are you getting a bit blind?
Your face has many wrinkles
hasn't it,
now you're getting old.
That's a nice walking stick
Can't you walk without it?
You will soon be thirty
won't you?

Jane Hitchman

very thin →

↑ Rinkels in his hands

Martin Farrer, 10

29

Adults just get drunk

If you are a grown-up you can do nearly anything you like, if it is not against the law. They can have parties, but they nearly always have a hang over. Sometimes grown-ups act stupid.   *Carol Peace, 10*

Grown-ups tend to have parties, not birthday parties because they hate to admit their age. The next morning there tends to be a few hangovers and the grown-ups sit in the kitchen staring at their breakfast as if it were going to kill them, and one slight noise and you're shushed at to be quiet. *Alison, 10*

Anthony Ferguson, 8

Mother is twenty-one again

My Mother keeps saying every year that she's twenty-one, but I'm getting a bit suspicious because she's said it for the last 12 years. *Gregory Payne, 11*

I love hassling my mother when it is her birthday. I keep reminding her that she is getting older and all I get is a clout on the ear! *Justin, 10*

Monday, 3rd April
Happy Birthday Old Girl!

Tuesday, 4th April
Appointment with the doctor — pain in back

Wednesday, 5th April
Appointment with dentist — false teeth fitted

Thursday, 6th April
Appointment with the optician
  — short sighted

Friday, 7th April
Bought a wheelchair

Saturday, 8th April
Appointment with the beauty
  therapist — removal of wrinkles

Sunday, 9th April
Appointment with God *Gabrielle, 14*

Christian Morton, 6

Cheer up Mom, we all get old. Just look at Dad.

Dale Fagence, 11

If we buy her a card with 16th birthday on the front, she says, "I like you, you can have extra pocket money".
Fiona Nicholls, 10

When it is my mother or father's birthday we usually give them chocolates so we can eat them. *Diane Allan, 11*

My mother said she doesn't mind *getting* older, it's *looking* older she can't stand.
Debbie Miano, 12

Cheer up Mum, don't be glum
Just think if there was no false teeth
All you would have is gums.
Patricia, 10

Although my mother is getting a little old she still likes to run wild on her birthday.
Gary Higson, 11

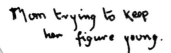

Mom trying to keep her figure young.

Caroline Weller, 8

YOU'RE GOING
BALD ON TOP

YOU'VE GOT
WRINKLES ON
YOUR FACE

YOUR JACKETS
BULGING
AT THE
SEAMS

YOUR FINGERS
ARE WORKED TO
THE BONE
YOUR FEET ARE
FULL OF BUNIONS

YOU'VE DONE A HARD

DAYS WORK SO .....

Sally Duckhoff, 13

Don't worry dad

YOU'RE NOT AS OLD
AS YOU LOOK

Poor old Dad!

Sometimes my Dad tries to hide that he is getting older and older each day, but he's not the world's best actor!
Harcus Roy Copper, 10

Happy birthday dear Dad. I see you're going bald, but never mind at least you won't get head lice.
Helen Lawrence, 10

It's Dad's birthday on Tuesday. Now what shall I get him? All his friends forgot last year and he was very sad. I'd like to forget my birthday especially if I was going to be *that* age.
Julie Wheeler

My Dad always gets money for his birthday. He's very rich and my Mom takes it away from him.
David Lyne, 7

Matthew Bebbington, 10

You know you are old when...

...you have a body like something out of Doctor Who.
Stuart Moore, 12

...you try to comb your hair so that it doesn't all fall out.
Patricia Mulqueen, 13

...you hang a sock on the fireplace and Santa ignores it.
Sandra Reddy, 14

...you start to say things like "In my day".
Carole Waters, 15

...you puff and pant when you've just been around the room with the vacuum cleaner. *Patricia Mulqueen, 13*

You know you're old when...
You're first at the station and last on the train,
but
You know you're really old when you're last in the doctor's waiting room,
but get wheeled to the front. *Kevin Doyle*

You know you're *really* old when you need new false teeth because your others are too worn down!
Jane McNeill, 13

Getting old is...getting white hairs from worrying about your wrinkles. *Sandra Reddy, 14*

You can tell when people get old. Their hair falls out and they get out of breath. They always talk about the old times and you haven't got a clue what they are talking about. *Mark Thornton, 11*

If they are very old they are born when the war starts.
Helen Anne Smith, 8

Rachel Hall, 8

The symptoms...

When you are old your body creaks and your knees knock and your teeth fall out.
Adrian Tydd, 10

...you get rincled skin and white hair and blood shot eyes.
Amanda Leonard, 11

...you get flopy.
Timothy Ferguson

...you might have false teeth.
Debbie White, 10

...you don't see so well.
Frank Bertelli, 15

...you might get a croaky voice.
Janine French, 8

Raymond Moore, 10

...you get very fat or you may get crumpled up.
Maurice Paine, 9

Also when you get old you will grow bent and shrink as well and you also seem to wear scarfs and hats.
Danny Field, 8

When you're grown up and you have a birthday you feel funny. You can't do PE any more because you can't bend over because of your fat tummy.
John Fielding, 8

you dont rush about When you are old your knees creak We can here you coming

Nigel Bosley, 10

It is natural for old people to get
smaller, not shrink really small in
just a few days, but for them to grow
smaller as the years go by.

Anne Baker, 11

...so you don't need to worry because
you don't have to bend down to get
into small cupboards   *Allan Sinfield, 8*

Old age is old men at a bar pinching young ladies
rear ends and old ladies needing hearing aids and
when they have got them in they still can't hear you.

David Ritchie, 10

Being old is not plesent. You have wobbly knees. You
have a crinckly face and a crinckly nose and your
eyes begin to shut. When it comes to birthdays you get
so excited your litly to have a hart attack.   *Nicky H.*

When you are an old man you go
all crooked and you keep falling
down

Paul Hewitson, 8

Old Fogies Anonymous

Remember the days you went to School, how you used to run after the girls and beat up the people who got on your nerves. Now your grandson is probably doing the same. But can you do the same now? Well I've never heard of anyone running with a walking stick.

Mario Marandola, 11

You are growing old at this second and by the time you have read this, you will be a few minutes older. Depressing, isn't it? But think of all the advantages. When you're a little old man or woman you can do whatever you like, say whatever you like and go wherever you like. If you're rude people won't mind, they'll just say you're old and your mind is wandering.

Sandra Marsden, 13

When you grow old you might feel lonely. On the other hand it might be nice to feel you have some authority over ruthless young children.

Cariad Seigle-Morris, 9

Old men make me think of cluttered up houses full of ancient golf clubs and books. *Emmeline Hiscocks, 10*

Old people can only normally be seen trapped inside their own little home with only a ferocious mean little dog for company, wrapped in clothes as if they were off on a polar expedition.

Stuart Moore, 12   *Samantha Syer, 7*

40

Getting older means a lot of things to me like meals-on-wheels, and bingo. But first the thing that strikes me most is wobly legs and bad backs. It also means becoming a grandfather or even a great grandfather, and if you have any children they become about thirty years old which makes you feel about four hundred.

Lee Caller, 11

People think of growing old like a disease you catch when you get to about sixty *Eamonn Brennan, 13*

Old ladies get mixed up with money. They give you a tiny coin and even though you won't be able to get a single ice cream you still say thank you. *Paul Hearne, 11*

What is old?
Old is telling people to do what
they're told. *Paul Healy, 12*

They say hello
and you say
hello back and
they yell out
WHAT!.

Rachel A. Fyfe, 10

Sarah Leonard, 6

Keep in shape old man!

Darren Forshaw, 9

Anthony Laws, 10

David James, 8

When they say you're over the hill, at least you can have some fun going down the other side

Andrew Chambers, 13

Louise Smith

Sarah Chadwick, 13

The grouchers

Older people are sometimes grouchy. Most of the time when they go along the street they talk to there selfs and mumbal. They are really fussy I can tell you that. You should hear them when my mother comes in, chitt chatt chatt, they go on and on.   *Helen, 9*

Old people complain a lot and are generally very noisy, interfering and old-fashioned. We have a lot to thank them for, so my mom says anyway.
                                                                       Joanna Summers, 13

I think old people are jealous of young people, although they may not realize it. There is an old lady who lives near me who thinks that whatever you do, you are the wrong age to do it. If you are going with your friends to a show, or a disco or something, she says you're too young. She sees you going to buy a toy though, then she says you're too old to have toys.
                                                                        Barbara Cains, 13

The Law

No old person may grouse.
No old person may pretend
to be deaf when you are carol
singing.
No old person may pretend
to not notice things.
No old person may bore you
to death by telling
you about when they were
young.
Anyone found guilty of
these crimes will not be able
to stand on a street and tut
"Kids" or anything like that.
                   Sean Scannell

◀ *Julian Harris, 6*   *David Oshor, 10*

Keep in shape and be stronger

Warren Tutty, 9

46

Oldies should do more sit-ups

My advice to everyone who wants to keep healthy. Jog for about one mile. If you can't jog, do some sit ups. About 400 every day.

Danny Leamon, 8

Paul Grey, 8

When my nana tries to touch her tooes she fell over and hurt her back.

Mandy Winters, 10

People shoad doow exercises so they keep looking young. If you don't you will get fat and your heart mit slow down and you will be ill and you mit dide.

Andrew Tomlinson, 8

Grandad goes for long walks to keep his legs in shape.

Mark Saunders, 11

Tracey Annal, 11

48

Never mind, poor old thing

Happy birthday all middle ages. Don't get so worried about getting old. You could even live in an old people's home where you'll have lots to do. You'll have outings and children sing Christmas carols at Christmas. So don't get worried. *Tracey Dixon, 9*

I hope you are well and have a nice birthday. Please live to next year.
From your little Monster. *John Johnson, 11*

P.S. I was going to send you some money, but I had already sealed the envelope.

If a person's teeth are falling out you could say, well at least you will be rich. You will get some money from the tooth fairy. Also you could exercise just by blowing out all the candles on your birthday cake every birthday. *Michael Amey, 10*

Growing old is what everyone is doing, though you may not think so. You are not going to age much when you are fifty or sixty but just realize that, in fact, you have been growing so old that it shows. *Katie Edgington, 14*

Oh! Antie Milly never mind about your wrinkly neck and your wrinkled face. I will still cuddle you and kiss you. You have lots of company because you are kind and the children who visit you don't mind one bite your shackey hands and a bite of your mastosh. *Donna Greenaway*

Did you go to the dentists on Wednesday, how many teeth did he take out? Oh that's alright if he only took out one. It was your last tooth? Oh well you can't win them all. *Michael Eastman, 11*

The deadly sins of old age

When I'm a grandma I won't start every sentence with, "When I was a girl".
Sarah Gardner, 14

When I'm very old, I won't make my grandchildren do as they're told, I'll spoil them rotten.
Tabitha Gardiner, 14

I won't pat my grandchildren on the head every time I see them and say, "My, how you've grown."
Dolores Marino, 14

When I am old I will not like pop music. It will give me a sore head. I will like soft music like hymns.
Roisin McGarry, 7

When I'm 92, I'll bore everyone by telling them how things cost nothing when I was a little girl. I'll tell them about life before computers.
Helena Rodriguez

When I'm older, I shall not grouse about the price of everything for hours on end.
Meryl Dellocano, 14

When I get older I'll not try to say what my grandma says: "I didn't do that when I was young" or "I didn't have one of those when I was young" or "I didn't say that to my parents when I was young I had a bit more respect".
Mary, 14

My resolution for when I get old is not to get old, I may age in years, but my brain and line of thought will continue to run as if nothing had happened. There is nothing worse than an elderly person who thinks they're old and continually complains about having a pain here and a pain there, etc. etc. Old age is in the mind.
Claire-Anne Logan, 14

Dominic Ashton, 7

We like the old ones

Really old people are terrific. They tell stories of their lives and are always saying "When I was young..."

Sarah Davison, 13

The happiest things about growing old are seeing again the beauty of spring, the browns, greens and falling leaves of autumn, and the feel of crisp snow in winter. It is also the joy of seeing grandchildren, great grandchildren and new young life, and teaching them and showing them the mysteries and wonders that each day brings.

Gillian Threadingham, 14

My great, great aunt is eighty-two. She sews a lot and hopes to live for a very, very long time so that she can finish all her sewing!

Zoë Upton, 9

Don't be offended if your daughter or son kids you about white hair, just say that it's silver and more valuable.

Katie Edgington, 14

Why do grandmas have to get older? Why can't they stay with their soft wrinkled skin? Why can't they stay with their old white hair?

Sara Ford, 11

I Lovit wen- they tell me wote theydid wen they wer Little.

Stuart Whittington, 7

52

When it is my Grandma's birthday she does not want it for the presents and the big dinner, but for the pleasure of seeing the family again.

Mark Anderson

People need people, but the longing is more in old age.

Jennifer Cowasji, 13

Grandparents like other peoples birthdays in a different way. They like people's birthdays if they now there happy. There happy to see the other person happy.

David Larkin, 9

Nina Wright

Grandparents are the greatest

My Grandma is terrific and kind. When my brother is horrible she gives him a clout.　　*Justine Kettle, 9*

When my dad shouts at me nana tells him to stop and then tells me all the bad things my dad used to do.
　　Dwayne Kimmel, 14

When I ask my grandma how old she is, she says I am as old as my fingers but a tiny bit older than my teeth. And we all laf.　　*Alison Ewan, 7*

My grandmother's birthday is a birthday with presents but without a number.　　*Sarah Parker, 11*

On her birthday she gets out her photograph albums and goes into a dream.　　*Zena Clay, 11*

My Grandma is getting older with wrinkles. All her knees are as nobbly as old potatoes, but I love my dear old Grandma as much as she loves me.
　　Andrew Broady, 8

My Grandma has a smile like the sun.　　*Martyn Scott, 7*

The most kindest wrinkled faced person I know is my nana. My nana is as old as the hills. You can tell by the wrinkles.　　*Marie Greenaway, 11*

Some grandmothers are very lovable. If we didn't have them we wouldn't be able to stay round their house and we wouldn't be spoiled.　　*Maureen Rooke*

My Nana is 50 but she's not grouchy though she plays with me. It's about when you reach 70 you're grouchy.
　　Clare Lansdown, 10

grandad and me

Sharon Fitzsimmons

I'll do roly-polys in the snow when I'm 87

<u>Is it fun at 87?</u>

I think I'll go wild when
I'm old and be quite eccentric.
Yes, I'd like that!
I'll go singing in the rain,
(something I've always wanted to do)
with bright yellow galoshes on and a red hat.
People don't mind what you do
When you're old, they just say,
"Poor old dear, she's not got long to go,"
And tap their heads.
So you see I could do all the things
I've always wanted to do,
but couldn't do,
because I was young.
Be like a little child at eighty-seven.
Jump in haystacks
And pick flowers from other people's gardens.
Do roly-polys in the snow.
I could have quite a bit of fun,
when I'm old.

Lisa Burnage, 14

James Davis, 12

56

The advantages...

When you are older you can swim better because booze makes you fat and you will float better.   *Samuel Ross, 8*

Look on the brighter side of being bald. At least you don't have to wash your hair any more.
Dara O'Connell, 13

At least when I'm old I won't have to put away all my toys every night.   *Billy Patulski, 10*

In a way it must be great to get old because you get an opportunity to stay in bed all day.   *Genevieve Wright, 10*

It must be great being a grandparent because however badly your grandchildren behave you can go home at the end of the day.   *Maria Sanchez, 14*

Everyone respects you and no one would have the heart to tell you to shut up when you started rambling on about what the old days were like for the umpteenth time.   *Susan Williams, 14*

You do not have to use your brains so much because they are a bit rusty.
    Karen Edwards, 10

Iain Jones, 7

Granma died when she was weard out

Mary

Mark Keene, 10

When they die
they will be burfed
in a Cafein and
when god comes
you will be ll Alive
and you
cam made a
cup of tea

Steven Blake

Young at heart

Some people think when they have those dreaded wrinkles they are old. That's crazy! It depends totally on you. You may not look the same but if you want you can act twenty years younger.

Cassandra Garner, 14

The first signs of growing old are eyes losing their innocence.

Justin Walker, 10

Old people are good at exagarating. But deep down they are young. There harts still containe love.

Stuart Berry, 9

When you grow older you look much different from when you were younger, but you might not *be* different.

Patrick Lord, 9

Wouldn't it be great if every one could live for ever especially Grandmas and Granddads because they bring lots of pleasure.

Angus Newhouse, 11

Sometimes on the news you hear of people who celebrate their 100th birthday by going up in Concorde or down in a submarine for the first time. Some young people would not do this. It's what you like not how old you are that matters.

Andrew Townsend, 11

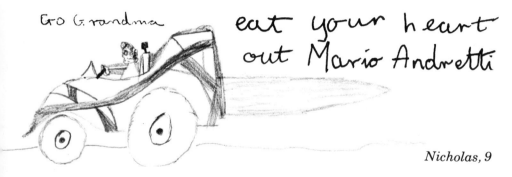

Nicholas, 9

Sharon Murphy, 6